Oper

GAME
PLAN

Operation GAME PLAN

**How to Overcome Habits That Hinder
Us From Succeeding in Life**

Chrys-Ann Ambrose

purposely
created
PUBLISHING

OPERATION GAME PLAN

Published by Purposely Created Publishing Group™

Printed in the United States of America

ISBN (ebook): 978-1-942838-65-4

ISBN (paperback): 978-1-942838-64-7

Special discounts are available on bulk quantity purchases by book clubs, associations and special interest groups. For details email: sales@publishyourgift.com or call (888) 949-6228.

For information logon to:
www.PublishYourGift.com

Dedicated to the masses, particularly the ten percenters—the ones that refuse to accept mediocrity, who push past the challenges of life and dare to become the success that they were born to be.

TABLE OF CONTENTS • • • • • • • • • • • • •

INTRODUCTION • • • • • • • • • • • • • • • • • •

Have you ever wondered what your life will be like in the future? Have you wondered if things will be better, how much you will achieve, and where you will be years from today? While some things in life are unpredictable and some circumstances are out of our control, the reality is many things are within our control. Whether we look at other peoples' lives and admire them for what they have achieved or we look at others and say we could never allow our lives to become that low, the truth is we have the power to become great and we have the power to remain as we are: lost, without direction and struggling to find our purpose.

This book will show how you can achieve the greatness that you dream of by putting the necessary plans in place. Life is an adventure that should be lived to the utmost. It should never be boring. As humans, we have the capacity and the ability to stretch ourselves to become the best that we can be. Unfortunately, we conform to what we see the masses do; we live their lifestyle because we decide to play it safe. For most of us, we make the decision to take the easy way out, not only because it's 'safe', but also because it's comfortable.

For many years, I stayed on the safe train. I lived my life like everyone else, doing what the masses did, never daring to be different. Even though I wanted to be successful in life, in my mind, success was for lucky people. I honestly believed people were born that way, and, to a certain extent, I was correct. What I believed at the time was that only successful people were born successful. One day, I got a rude awakening. I realized EVERYONE was born successful.

What determined if they remained that way was they themselves!

In this book I will explain the facts as I discovered them over a period of between 5 and 7 years. I cannot promise you that after reading this book that your success will take off by leaps and bounds; that will totally depend on you and how you receive the information and what you do with it, if you decide to do anything. I am not an expert on psychology, nor do I hold any degrees from any university. The information I am sharing with you is information I have learned from spending time with successful people and reading books that were recommended by people who are in their lives where I wanted to be in my own. These are my experiences and things that I have learned and applied to my life that worked for my family and me.

Be prepared to be amazed by the simple knowledge that can change your life, once you decide to apply it. The information is simple; the hard part is the application. As difficult as it may be, I encourage you to develop a habit of consistency once you make the decision to change your life. The decision of success is always yours.

In the words of my mentor and life coach, Brenda Cotto, here's 'to your amazing success'.

Chrys-Ann

CHAPTER 1

THE GAME PLAN

"If you don't design your own life plan, chances are you'll fall into someone else's plan. And guess what they have planned for you? Not much." - Jim Rohn

What's the game plan?

The Cambridge English Dictionary's definition is 'a plan for achieving success'. The term 'game-plan' is usually applied to sports, but I am going to apply it to your life. What is the game plan for your life? Sadly, most people lack a plan of action for their lives. I fell into that category for years. For most people, their game plan is based on what the masses do: go to school, get an education, get a job, pay bills, and then die.

I know it sounds a bit morbid, but the sad fact is that most of us don't know any differently, so we settle for what everyone else is doing. We look at the smart few who take the road less traveled and we think of how great, brilliant, and lucky they are.

The truth is, the only things that separate them from us are their game plan, their willingness and their discipline to follow through. Here's a fact that we need to be aware of.

Every life has a game plan and we are in life where we allow ourselves to be. The cold hard truth is this: If we do not take charge and put a plan in place for our lives, one will be put in place for us. I cannot promise you that you will like the game plan that you are handed. Your circumstances will be totally out of your control until you decide to do something about them.

Think about it.

Can you imagine how things would be if your circumstances, your boss, and your peers controlled the outcome of your life? Those are just to name a few. Living your life without a game plan would be the equivalent of jumping into a boat without any sails, oars or an engine and just hoping that you will arrive at your destination in record time. Seriously, does that make much sense? To a crazy person, maybe. So what makes us think that we can just go about life, doing the same average things day in and day out and hoping that maybe we will end up successful? My point exactly. You have to think about how you really want your life to be, put some plans in place, and stick to them until you achieve your goals. I am not going to promise you that once you put the plans in place, everything will work out perfectly. The game plan is simply the strategy or plan that you use to map out your life. Once your game plan has been mapped out, the next step is to execute it. Knowing what you want to do with your life is only half the battle. Doing it is the other half. Where we are in life is entirely up to us.

To be honest, for years I found it extremely easy to blame circumstances for where I was in life. I was at a dead end job doing the same thing day in and day out. The sad thing was I honestly thought that life would get better *some day*. I bought into the lie that some day my ship would come in. I even had the nerve to feel sorry for myself because no opportunities were coming my way. I know many people are currently in that situation, doing the same thing daily, hoping that *one day* things will change, *one day* things will get better ... one day.

Here's the thing: we are in control of our 'one day'. We can decide when that day will come. We are in life where we choose to be. Do yourself a favor: Take the reins and steer your life in the direction you want to go. It is futile and downright insane to be doing the exact same things over and over and over again expecting different results. If something is not working, the logical thing to do is fix it. It starts with a decision. Where do you want to go? What do you want to do? If you know where you want to go and what you want to do, start putting the plans in place to get there.

UNSURE?

If you are not sure what you want to do with your life, it's time for some soul searching. This may take a bit of time, but it has to be done. From experience, I've found that it helps to mentally step out of yourself and view your life as someone else's. I know it sounds strange, but here's a fact about us humans: we tend to be perfect judges and advisors when it comes to other peoples' lives. For example, have you ever taken a look at someone and said to yourself that he or she is wasting their life, or that they have so much going for themselves and are wasting their opportunities? How about doing that for yourself? Visualize your life as someone else's. Look at the talents and opportunities you have in your own life. Trust me. You *do* have talents and opportunities. We all do. Here's an assignment. Ask yourself for advice on what to do with your life. What advice would you give yourself? It is highly unlikely that you would not have an answer.

Try it for yourself. It will work, but here's the important thing.

You MUST take yourself seriously. It may take you a bit of time to complete this exercise, but I advise you to stick with it until you get answers. I would also suggest that you get a journal and write everything down. Every talent, every opportunity, every possibility should be written down. Take this exercise very seriously. This is your future that you're dealing with; handle this with kid gloves. Once you come up with an answer, start putting plans in place to take your dream forward. You may need to consult with an expert in that particular field. There is also lots of online help that you can get in the form of search engines and videos. Utilize today's technology. Let it be your slave.

LOOK TO THE FUTURE

Because daily life can become mundane and habitual, it's very easy to live from day to day and not think of the future. Before we know it, years turn into decades and one day we wake up to the realization that we have not done anything to make our future better.

The future has a habit of sneaking up and surprising the present out of us.

In order to avoid disappointment in how life turns out, we need to prepare for our future now.

Sadly, a big misconception we have is that we have time.

Don't fall into that trap.

The things we do today and every day will determine how we live later on.

Keep the future in mind every day and build on it daily. The little things that are done daily DO add up. If you decide you want a degree in a particular field but you tell yourself that it will take too long, I suggest that you start now. Five years will pass whether you work on the degree or not. It would be much better to come out at the end of five years with the degree than without it. The future is going to happen whether or not you participate in it. You, however, control which end of the success tunnel you come out of.

Your past should not be the boss of your future

Whatever happened in the past has already happened. I highly doubt that it can be undone.

While lots of people were born into a life that had their future paved for them and already mapped out with success, the reality is that many more were not born with these advantages.

Whatever difficulties we had growing up should not be indicators of how or where we later end up. If someone grew up in a dysfunctional family and had a string of ancestors who never graduated from high school, much less college, that individual has the final say on whether his or her life will continue on that pattern or not.

There is a powerful tool called choice that determines whether or not a person becomes successful.

Great news! EVERYONE has that tool.

Sad news! Not everyone uses it to his or her advantage. Unfortunately, I have seen too many people second guess themselves because of their past.

Today, make the choice to break the cycle of mediocrity. Stop using the past as a boulder in your path to success. If your past hinders you from progress, then that's your choice. You have the powerful weapon of choice. Use it and choose well.

LENA'S STORY

My daughter and her best friend, Lena, attended the same high school. Even though she is two years younger than my daughter, they were inseparable. I constantly refer to them as my twin daughters. One thing I noticed throughout the years was they were inseparable until end-of-term exams. During that time, Lena would be missing in action until school went on holidays. At first I found it a bit strange until I realized what was really happening. Lena had a game plan for her life and she was determined that no one was going to distract her from it.

The funny thing was, it took me years to figure it out. I simply thought that her parents demanded good grades or else, and she was doing whatever it took to stay in their good graces.

At least, that's what it looked like on the surface.

On the surface, Lena seemed like an average teenage girl. The youngest of five children, she played football with my daughter and had a seemingly normal life. What I did not realize at the time was that Lena's parents instilled a discipline in her that would make her successful.

While most girls her age were hanging out on the weekends, watching television or playing video games, Lena was dedicating at least five hours daily to her school work.

On the days that she played football, she spent extra hours studying, as her parents threatened to take her off the team if her grades fell below an A. It was Lena's dream to become an oncology surgeon, so she concentrated on her science subjects because she knew they would be required for her to be accepted into medical school. In her final year of high school, Lena had her game plan in place.

She knew her parents were unable to afford the tuition for medical school, so she worked extremely hard to maintain an A average, particularly in chemistry and physics. By doing this, she graduated at the top of her class and was able to secure a scholarship at the local medical school. Within her first year of university, she received an award for being the top student in chemistry. One year later, she began her pre-med program.

Night after night, Lena could be seen on her verandah with her lap top studying into the wee hours of the morning, after getting home from her classes sometimes as late as 10:00 p.m.

During her summer break from school, while everyone else took that opportunity to relax and unwind, Lena decided to spend that time working with her aunt in the United States who was an oncologist.

A few months after the new semester, our island was hit by a hurricane and there was no power for almost a week. While the university had a back-up power plant, no one else on our street had a generator with the exception of a nearby building. The building had a parking area that was lit by a generator while the entire neighborhood was in total darkness. It was not until Lena returned to a dark house after enjoying the comfort of her generator-lit classroom that she realized she had a problem.

How was she to study in the dark? Deciding that a dark house was not going to break her study routine, she dragged a chair and table along with her laptop over to the generator lit parking area and did her regular study time.

This went on night after night with her older brother and sister standing guard while Lena battled the mosquitoes to put in her regular study time. Eventually, after about a week, the power company was able to complete repairs to the downed power lines and restore the electricity to our neighborhood.

I will never forget this example of dedication and commitment to a game plan.

Lena was completely sold out to her game plan despite the circumstances and setbacks. While making my observations over the years, one thing that stood out most to me is that success is not easy. One mentor explained to me that success is never meant to be easy. If it were easy, most people would be successful. The key to producing a successful game plan is having the dedication required to stick to it. As expected, life can be unpredictable, and there are setbacks.

Later on in this book, we will look at how to handle the setbacks and other unexpected surprises that life throws at us. One important lesson that I have learned is that we must never allow unexpected circumstances to deter us from our game plan. If you are walking on the road to success and you encounter a roadblock, you must either climb over it or find a detour around it. Like I said earlier, success was never meant to be easy; if it was, more of us would be successful.

CHAPTER 2

YOU WERE BORN A SUCCESS

"Most men are beaten with the rods of their own making"
- Unknown

Yes, you were born a success. We all were born successes. I understand if this shocks you, because I was just as shocked when I heard it. It does not matter if you were born limbless, you were born a success. And here's the other shocker: you will die a success. You see, when we were born, we were born fearless. We were born believing that we can do anything.

Observe babies. They are the most confident people in the world. They believe they can do anything. They believe that they can defy the law of gravity. They even believe that they can walk on water. That's how we were born.

However, things change as we grow up. Little by little, restrictions are introduced to us and we learn to conform. If you wrap a baby up comfortably and give him a bottle and put him to sleep in a graveyard, I guarantee you he would sleep comfortably throughout the night. He may wake up for a diaper change, but the thought of sleeping in a graveyard would not bother him one bit. Then as he grows, some smart person would put thoughts in his head about dead people and ghosts, and I can guarantee you that you would never get him to sleep in a graveyard after that.

The point I am making is that when we were born, we had a clean slate. Our minds were untouched. The only belief we had was that we could do anything. There were no restrictions in our minds whatsoever. We were not yet introduced to 'can't' and 'fear' and other debilitating words.

Please don't misunderstand me. I understand that rules are put in place to protect us, and I respect those rules. What I am saying is that society and associations mold our minds and make us who we are. Do you remember that you had the biggest dreams when you were a child? As children, we were ten feet tall and bulletproof. In our minds, we were going to have the best jobs, own the biggest homes, drive the best cars, and wear the best clothes. Then somewhere along the line as we matured, our dreams went from ten feet tall to only inches high, and we began to accept the mediocre lives that we live. What happened? I'll tell you what happened. We conformed. We listened to people's advice that 'life is not easy' and 'you can't do that because ...' or, even worse (and I know this one will strike a nerve), we followed the patterns of our parents and the people around us.

Think about it. If there is a generational pattern of no one in the family going to university, chances are that the pattern will continue for generations to come until someone decides to change that pattern. The sad thing is that, because they lack belief, most people do not recognize the greatness and success within them. For many years I believed this lie. I stayed in a dead-end job, believing that it was my lot in life and that I was no better so I deserved no better. Here's what I have to tell you. STOP BELIEVING THE LIE! Yes. That is exactly what it is: a lie.

I remembered that someone loaned me a CD and I listened to it during the ten-minute drive to work one day. The information that I heard was amazing. I remembered the presenter saying that rich people teach their children that they can do anything in life they set out to accomplish. She said that they constantly feed positive information to their children and remove all the limits from their lives.

I remember sitting in my car when I arrived at work listening to those words and the first thing I thought was, 'What a bunch of hogwash. How can I possibly achieve greatness by just believing?' The funny thing was that even though I thought she was spewing fairy dust, I listened to the CD over and over again. She spoke about changing associations, getting around people who were in life where I wanted to be. She even named books and suggested that listener get their hands on them and study them. I remember that this was the moment that changed my life because as unreal as it sounded, I decided to give it a try. I got my hands on as many books as I could and I not only read them, I studied them. I also listened to CDs.

After a while, something strange happened—I started believing in myself. After decades of living a mediocre life, believing that I was average, believing that I did not deserve to be great, I actually felt good about myself. I finally felt that I was worth something. Anyway, enough about me. Let me teach you what I learned.

The only limits on your life are the ones that you set. Yeah, that's right. We set the limits. We decide how far we go in life and how successful we become. Listen to me. Stop allowing yourself to keep you back. I understand that there are obstacles in our lives that hinder our progress, but here's the cold hard fact on obstacles: Obstacles only become obstacles if we allow them to be obstacles. Let me break it down for you. This may probably be the longest chapter in this book because there are so many things that we allow to hinder our growth. I cannot touch on them all, but I will cover the most common ones that can and will keep you from progressing with your game plan.

FEAR AND ANGER

Here are two emotions that are constantly misused: fear and anger.

When we fear, we tend to run from the very thing that scares us, and I understand that. If there is a dangerous situation, we should run from it. What I cannot understand though is this:

Why in tarnation do we think that we should run from success? Why do we fear it? Why do we run from the very thing that we were born with that will take us to higher levels? It seems to be a common thing for people to fear and run from success but embrace and accept poverty and mediocrity. As I write this, I am shaking my head because I was just as guilty of this. Maybe in your mind you are telling yourself that you do not fear success, but you are afraid to step out and take a chance because you are afraid of failure. And I get that. I really do. Here is the problem with that. Your fear of failure, which keeps you from taking chances, is the very thing that may keep you mediocre for the rest of your very life, and if you're okay with that, that's fine. However, if you're tired of being stuck in the same box that you put yourself in, now is the perfect time to get out. I will talk some more about the 'box' a little later in this chapter.

Everyone feels fear. Even great people, and from here until the end of this book, when I refer to great or successful people, I mean people who utilized the greatness they were born with. The difference is that great people don't let their fear stop them from taking action, and even though they are afraid, they move forward. Maybe you want to start a business or pursue a degree or write a book. You may be afraid of failing. You may say to yourself, "What if I invest my money and I fail? What if I go off to pursue my degree and I fail? What if I write a book and I fail?" Let me ask you a question: What if you don't fail? Why don't you ask yourself, "What if I succeed?" The fear of success may be another fear. Let me give you a piece of advice: Do not allow fear to stop you from progressing. If you have a dream, put a game plan in place and follow it to the very end. If you do not pursue your dream, it will haunt you for the rest of your life. You will always wonder to yourself what would have happened if only you had the courage to step out. Even if you fail, DO NOT think of yourself as a failure. Just pick yourself up, dust yourself off, and try again. There are no great or successful people who have never failed. Even Thomas Edison, the inventor of the light bulb, failed 1500 times before he succeeded. What would have happened if he gave up? Either we would still be working by candlelight or someone else would have continued the quest to invent the light bulb and received the credit. NEVER allow fear to hold you back. Even if failure occurs, use it as a stepping stone to success.

A NEGATIVE MINDSET

As humans, we were not born with a negative mind. Our minds were molded that way. A negative mindset is a dangerous and destructive mind. Unfortunately, it is easier to maintain a negative mind than a positive mind. We have practiced being negative for so long that negative thinking has become a habit that we are not even aware of. It has become second nature. The good news is that as habits are learned and formed, they can become unlearned and unformed. The bad news is that negative thinking is a very difficult habit to break, but remember that I said earlier that success is not easy; if it were, more people would be successful. For most of us, we grew up in a society hearing and believing negative talk day in and day out. That negativity became embedded in our minds and created our negative habits. I learned quite a bit while studying many books on how the mind works.

Let me try and make this simple. There is the conscious mind and the subconscious mind. The conscious mind is composed of the things that we are aware of, such as the colour of the sky, what we pay attention to, etc. However, the subconscious mind works on a deeper level. It picks up information that we are not even aware of and stores this information away. While our conscious mind shuts off when we are sleep, the subconscious mind keeps working. It never takes a break. Our conscious mind may be limited by the amount of information that it can take in at one particular time. That is why when we listen to a speaker, for example, we retain only a certain amount of information. The subconscious mind, however, keeps taking in information long after our conscious mind shuts off. It also has a way of later bringing up that information that it stores. Our habits and behaviors are results of our subconscious mind.

When we are constantly bombarded with negativity on a daily basis, our conscious mind takes in as much as it can and we constantly think negatively. The remainder of the information gets sucked into our subconscious. While our conscious mind can decipher truth from fiction, our subconscious mind cannot. It takes EVERYTHING as fact.

Is there any wonder why all we think and breathe is negative? We are so habitually negative that if we receive ten compliments and only one negative statement in one day, we automatically shelf the ten compliments and lament the only negative statement. If we are having a bad day, we totally forget about all of the good things that are happening and concentrate on the two bad things. Here's the honest truth about life: No matter how bad things are, there are always more things going right than wrong. The sad fact is, because of how our minds are wired, we only see the bad.

In a world that seems to be falling apart, we need to start feeding our minds more positive information. When we feed our minds positive food, our subconscious mind will pick up the remainder of the positive food that our conscious minds left over and little by little, it will bring forth the positive information. Like I said earlier, this will seem a little difficult at first, so let's take baby steps. If you make it a daily habit to read the negative events taking place in the world, or if you constantly listen to the news every chance you get, try limiting the amount of negative information you expose yourself to. Trade some of your 'news' time for time spent reading something positive. Little by little, your mind will start the adjustment. Another thing I learned was that the mind cannot think two thoughts at the same time.

Whenever you are tempted to think a negative thought, try replacing it with a positive one. The first time I tried doing this, it felt like I was trying to pull my hair out. I quickly realized how much the mind loves negativity. Has anyone ever angered you and it just satisfied you to rant to another person about how much that person offended you? Or how about this one: Have you ever been in a group discussion about how hard things are or how difficult life is? It's not so easy to separate yourself from the negative crowd and go in the opposite direction to positivity.

As difficult as it is, in order to achieve your success, it must be done. You need to speak positive thoughts to yourself over and over and over again. You need to forget all of the lies that you were told about not having what it takes to get ahead in life. Everyone has what it takes to get ahead because they were born with it. Too often, people die with talents left untapped and undeveloped. It's time to break free from the negative habits that hold you back. It's time to break the chains with which you have imprisoned yourself and move forward. Yes, you chained yourself. Someone may have handed you the chains, but you were the one who took them and imprisoned yourself. Stop believing the lie that you will never amount to anything greater. I want you to get some 3 x 5 cards and write positive affirmations on them and read them aloud to yourself every day. EVERY DAY! NO CHEATING! If you don't know what to write, here are a few things to start with:

I can do this.

I have what it takes.

I was born with greatness within me.

I am the only one who can stop me from doing this.

I am a winner.

I AM successful.

Once you decide to change your mindset, start feeding your mind positive food and start learning. You will never be the same again. Here's why: Once you have stretched your mind, it can NEVER return to its original size. It will never go back to normal.

ASSOCIATIONS

To truly move ahead, you may need to change your associations. I am not suggesting that you immediately kick all of your friends to the curb. But if you are going to be great at anything, you will need to limit the time you spend with negative-minded people. You will be deterred by many of the people you associate with as you share your dreams with them. Some people will mean well when they offer their advice. They may tell you that now is not the right time, the economy is bad, and on and on the advice will go. Some advice may come from your very good friends who want you to remain average with them because they are not ready to move forward in life.

My experiences were the same. Some of my so-called friends just wanted me to remain on the same level as they were because they did not want to change their own lives. I later learned this simple sentence to be true: You can tell where someone will be in five years by the books they read and the people they associate with. I also observed for years that successful people always associate with successful people. This is not because they think that they are better than average people. It's because in order to become and remain successful, you must always be in a state of learning. You learn success from successful people.

Let's take a drug addict, for example. Whenever a drug addict makes the decision to get help, he goes through a withdrawal stage when he is taken away from his fix. After he completes his drug program, he is warned to stay away from his old associations, his former fellow drug addicts and drug dealers. If he stays with positive people who will encourage him, there is a high possibility that he will remain sober. If he goes back to the old way of life, hangs around the users and pushers, he will probably fall back into the same habits. Many times, drug addicts stick with their new positive associations and turn their lives around.

Only later on in life, when their new mindsets become engrained in them, they return to their old stomping ground to help their old associations get sober. Once we make the decision to become successful, we must be very careful about associations. The decision to help others to become successful is a great one. At the same time, we must be sure to affect them in a positive way and not have them re-infect us with their negativity. The sad thing is that as much as we may want to help everyone that we know, not everyone will welcome the help, as sometimes the pain of changing becomes greater than the pain of remaining the same.

THE COMFORT ZONE

Let's talk about the box I mentioned earlier in this book. In life, we are taught to conform. We are told that there is only so far in life that we can go. We get put in the proverbial box and told to stay there. Whether we are told by society and circumstances or we tell ourselves, we are told that this is what it is— get in your box and stay there. So we climb into our little box and we get comfortable, and that's where we stay.

That box is the comfort zone. We don't have to stretch ourselves or get uncomfortable. We just get comfortable being average. We look around us and all of our associations are in their little boxes and they are comfortable. Here's the thing: Everyone is in a box. It's just that some boxes are larger than others. Here's the other thing: Some people have changed boxes many times and they have changed to a bigger box every time. Successful people are the ones who constantly upgrade to bigger boxes. They are the ones who continually step out of their comfort zones to upgrade their lives. They ask the tough questions, seek information about how to get to where they want to go, and do what it takes whether they are in the mood or not. Once you make the decision to become successful, the comfort zone will seek you out and try to pull you back in. You may even step back into your box and tell yourself that you will continue later, and that's okay. The only problem with this is that you do not want to stay in the comfort zone for too long. You will quickly want to develop another habit: getting uncomfortable.

Moving forward in life takes a level of discomfort. Turning off the television or putting down the controls for the Xbox and getting productive is never easy. Changing those habits will take some time, but the trick is to stay consistent in developing that habit of being productive. Always remember that you can never sit in your comfort zone and do your best. In order to give something your best shot, you must get uncomfortable. It takes lots of courage to leave the comfort zone. Unfortunately, most people never do.

PROCRASTINATION

Quite a big word and a powerful weapon that we use against ourselves is 'procrastination'. Here's my very accurate definition of procrastination: to defer action until an opportunity is lost. The comfort zone is a big culprit for this one. Once we get comfortable, we decide that we can get to the task later. The problem with this is that it can become habitual. Once procrastination becomes a habit, it becomes very difficult to break. The other dangerous thing is that we fool ourselves into believing that we will actually get to the task later.

However, once we get into that habit of constantly deferring action, the task will never ever get done. Good intentions are not actions and will never be. If you are a student and you have an exam in one week, you know that you need to study. If you keep putting off studying every day for a whole week, you will never study, and chances are you will fail the exam. For most people, opportunities pass by like a full bus because they fail to act. Procrastination is full of good intentions and no action. It will never get you past thinking. Kick it out the door of your mind. It is a casket that will keep you dead to success.

EXCUSES

Personally, I have zero tolerance for excuses. At one time in my life, I used them constantly to remain in my comfort zone when the pain of changing became too great for me to manage. Eventually, I realized that excuses were nothing but lies with a good reason. Making excuses is the same as lying to yourself. The sad thing is that too often we believe the lies. We actually believe that the excuses are valid. When we want to remain in our comfort zone a little longer or we want to procrastinate, we find a good reason to lie to ourselves. I often say to people that when we decide that we really want success as much as we want to breathe air, we will eliminate every excuse from our little black book of lies posing as reasons. Thomas J. Smith once said, 'Excuses are tools of incompetence used to build monuments of nothingness, and those who specialize in them seldom accomplish anything'. The thing is that anyone can come up with an excuse at any time for anything. I am not talking about an emergency. Emergencies should only delay us and never deter us. Life happens, and yes, there are setbacks, but never should we allow anything to permanently stop us in our tracks while we are on the road to success.

Remember the suggestion I made about replacing a negative thought with a positive one? Here's another exercise and habit to develop. Whenever you try to lie to yourself about why you can't complete a positive action that will move you closer to being successful, try this: replace the excuse with this thought 'I'm doing this'. Whether you feel like it or not, get up and talk to yourself. Tell yourself that you are going to do this (whatever 'this' may be for you at that time) and start moving. If you have a meeting to attend and don't feel like going, and all you want to do is to call and cancel and make up some flimsy excuse about why you can't make it, get up, put your shoes on, and pick up your supplies. Even though all the while your mind is screaming at you and telling you not to go, tell yourself that you are doing this; grab your keys and walk out the door. Scream at yourself if you have to, but for goodness sake, shut out the lazy voice in your mind that is telling you that you're too tired or that it's raining so you can't be successful today. Lies! These are all lies that we convince ourselves are truths. We even tell ourselves that now is not the right time. Newsflash!

Success is never convenient. There is never a convenient time to be successful. If we continue to listen to the lying reasons of excuses, we will never become successful. Kick them out the door along with procrastination.

SELF-PITY

This is one of the most unconstructive things we can carry. Self-pity is like sitting in a rocking chair for hours, rocking back and forth. It takes all of your energy and gets you nowhere. It wastes your time. In my case, I had a very negative outlook on life and I did not see things getting any better for me. I wallowed in self-pity and blamed the world for my lack of progression in life, not realizing that I was the one holding myself back. I invested years in this ridiculous practice. My favorite song was 'woe is me' and 'nobody knows the trouble I've seen' (pathetic). And what did it get me? Depressed. Where did it get me? Nowhere! That's exactly what I mean. Self-pity is unconstructive; it keeps you focused on what you don't have and not what you do have, and that in itself is a tragedy. It keeps you blind to the millions of things going right in your life and keeps you focused instead on the few things that are not going your way.

Self-pity is destructive. It totally destroys any chance of progression. It is always accompanied by negative thoughts. When we sit in that rocking chair totally focusing on every single negative thing in our lives, we fully block any little chance we may have of focusing on a solution. I mentioned earlier that the mind cannot hold two thoughts at once. When self-pity becomes a habit, it becomes comfortable for us because we have already adjusted ourselves and our minds to the routine. We have also adjusted our minds to blocking any solution to the problem. We don't do this deliberately; we do it habitually. If someone tries to help us overcome the problem, we habitually block the solution with an excuse. Remember, an excuse is a lie disguised as a reason, so we will fool ourselves into believing that the excuse is a valid reason.

If we are determined (habitually) to be unhappy, we will be, no matter what anyone else does to help us. In order to break out of it, we have to break the habit, and in order to break the habit, we have to want to break the habit. I know that it sounds strange, but truthfully, it has to start with our determination to want that change. Once that determination is made, then we need to get into that habit of focusing on positive thoughts and solutions. Shoot down every negative thought with a positive one and totally eliminate ALL excuses. Develop the habit of thinking positively on purpose, don't wait to feel like it. It's time to get up off of the rocking chair and progress in life. Self-pity is NOT worth the effort it requires. All it does is wear you out.

BEING TOO BUSY

Here's the million-dollar question. What are you busy doing? There is a huge difference between being busy and being productive. Sometimes we're so busy and at the end of the day, we have no idea what we did all day. We have to decide what it is we want to spend most of our time accomplishing. If you're so busy trying to complete a million tasks in a day, chances are by the end of the day, you will have completed your day accomplishing nothing. What we need to do is ask ourselves, 'What is important?'

Everything that we do in life either affects the present or the future. For example, if we spend the entire day cleaning our car or house, we will presently have a clean car or house. It mostly affects the present. If we spend an entire day investing in ourselves whether it's reading a positive book or training ourselves for our future career, we are committing an act now that will affect our future in a positive way. While we are so busy with activity, the important thing is to be busy with future-based activities, which are activities that will affect us positively for years to come.

I am in no way saying that we should not clean our homes or cars. What I am saying is that we need to invest a significant amount of time doing the things that will get and keep us on the road to success. This will be discussed in more detail later in the book when we get to the chapter dealing with time management.

These are just a few things that we allow to hinder our progress. The most important thing to realize is that we get what we allow in life. I am fully aware that many things in life are beyond our control, but the truth is that we have more control than we think. We can control what we allow to take place in our minds. Promise yourself that from this day forward, you will not allow any negative thought, habit, or person to hamper your progress in life. Wherever we are in life is where we allow ourselves to be. Develop a healthy habit of believing that you deserve the very best. Once you believe that, then you're on your way.

CHAPTER 3

YOUR HABITS BECOME YOUR LIFE

"We are what we repeatedly do. Excellence, then, is not an act, but a habit" - Aristotle

Wikipedia.org defines habit as "a routine behavior that is repeated regularly and tends to occur unconsciously." Our daily habits did not just start yesterday. We have been practicing what we do daily for most of our lives, from walking and talking to our dietary habits and beyond. When we first learned to walk, we were very aware because with every few steps we took, we took a fall or two. After mastering that art, we now do it without even thinking about it.

The habits we practice, whether good or bad, happen the exact same way. We are so programmed that we perform them without even thinking. If we take a step back and look at our lives, we will see that we are in life where our habits have taken us. I am not saying that circumstances don't have a part to play, because they definitely do. What I am saying is that we are in life where we put ourselves based on what we do habitually on a daily basis.

Let's break this down a little further. Most of us grew up believing that we would be successful. Now that we are adults, we are not as successful as we believed we would become. What happened? Our habits happened. It's one thing if you want to climb a mountain but you physically can't, and another thing when you can but you do nothing to even get yourself close to the base of the mountain to begin to climb it. Every habit that we have in life has results. If you have a habit of cleaning your house daily, then the result of that habit will be a clean house. If you habitually brush your teeth daily, then the result of that habit will be healthy teeth.

Just as good habits yield good results, bad habits yield bad results. The same will also apply for constructive habits and destructive habits. Ask yourself this question and be honest with yourself, 'Where are my daily habits taking me?' As you become honest with yourself, you may realize that your habits are keeping you from a successful life. That's okay. Don't be too hard on yourself at this point.

It is highly likely that you never realized it. That is the thing with a habit once it has been developed to perfection; it becomes an unconscious action. What you need to do now is cultivate the habits that will now take you forward. I will warn you that this is not going to be easy for the first few days or maybe even the first couple of weeks. What you need to do is start slow. If you are a person who can take giant leaps of progression and stick with it without any problems, then by all means, do it. For the rest of us, we may need to get used to a new habit one step at a time.

Our comfort zone also plays a big part with habits. When we become comfortable with our habits, changing them means we are stepping outside of our comfort zone. It will be painful at first, but as you practice daily, it gets easier. I like to compare it with wearing braces on your teeth. Here's my experience with this. When I first got fitted for braces, the discomfort was unbearable. I had a few teeth that were a bit crooked, so I knew that in order for me to have a 'Hollywood' smile I had to bear the pain and discomfort. Here's the other thing, while most people with braces used the metal type that could only be removed by the dentist, I opted for the clear removable ones that I could remove and replace whenever I wanted. However, despite the pain and discomfort, I kept them on for most of the day, only removing them to eat and brush my teeth. After the first week or so, the pain became less and less, and I was able to keep them on without any discomfort whatsoever. I did not notice much change when I looked in the mirror, but I knew that something had to be changing because there was absolutely no pain 3 to 4 weeks after.

The time came when I had to go back to the dentist for an adjustment. Because my teeth had moved a fraction, I was fitted with another set of braces to move them a fraction closer to the desired results. Again, there was pain, but I stayed consistent with keeping the braces on despite the pain. A week later, the pain lessened and three weeks later as my teeth got comfortable with their new position, I was pain free. At this point I was able to see subtle changes in the position of my teeth. I was elated. After 2 months of pain, I saw progress.

However, that progress was not the goal. The goal was to have a 'Hollywood' smile. So the process was repeated month after month for 3 years, and every month was the same. It started off painful but got easier with repetition. At the end of each month, my teeth got straighter and straighter until I reached that goal and attained my 'Hollywood' smile.

If you noticed from this analogy, my teeth were done gradually and not instantly straightened to achieve immediate results. If it was done that way, the nerves would be damaged and I would have lost my teeth. Nice, straight teeth were the goal here and not dentures. It works the same way with changing a habit. Good and constructive habits are only formed with daily practice. You know your limits, so stick to them when doing this. If the process is rushed, then you will automatically fall back and convince yourself that you cannot do it. When stretching your comfort zone, you need to do it gradually until you arrive at that level. After you get comfortable with that level, stretch yourself some more.

Thinking success with no action

One of the things that you don't want to do is arrive at the decision that you need to develop good habits and do nothing to start the process. Procrastination creeps in almost immediately when a decision is made to move forward. We tell ourselves that we will get to it tomorrow or we will wait until the new year to start fresh. What you need to do is start your baby steps immediately. Immediate action is required to throw procrastination out the door. Evict it from your life as soon as possible, because it is one sure way to keep you stagnant in life. Even after beginning with your new habit, procrastination will tell you that you did a good and consistent job for two days, so you are deserving of a break. Because developing new habits is such a fragile process, you will take that break and two days will become three and before you know it, you're back into the old habit.

Procrastination is a killer habit that will annihilate your progress and keep you stagnant. It is one habit that you will want to annihilate before it annihilates your success.

Thinking success and thinking action

While it's easy to assume that thinking success is the start to moving forward, it is not the only thing that will get you there. If you want to be a professional basketball player, it will help you to not only see yourself playing professional basketball, but also to study professional basketball players, their moves, their stats, and their techniques. However, if all you do is sit on the couch, study professional basketball videos, and watch the games, you will never become a professional in that field. You can even spend all day with a professional and talk game until the sun goes down and rises again the following day, and all you will have is the knowledge. It takes physical work to achieve that dream.

For too long I have observed people saying that they are going to do this and that with their lives. Time passes and years later, they are still at the same place. It's the same thing with positive and constructive habits. Get into the habit of working and exercising your physical habitual muscles. Thinking, saying, and learning will get you only so far. The real progress comes when you get up off the couch and start doing. Thinking success + thinking action + physical action = success. Don't shortcut the process. If you do, you will shortchange yourself. Being successful depends on what we do daily. That, my friend, is the secret to success.

Future based or present based?

When analyzing our habits, we need to observe which habits keep us stagnant and which ones move us forward. As I mentioned earlier, if you have a habit of cleaning your house daily, the result will be a clean house. At the same time, cleaning house is a present-based action that will only affect the present. Let's look at the habit of a drug addict. We all know that drug use is a bad habit. Here's the question. Is it present based or future based? Some will argue that it is only present based because the 'high' only lasts for a short while. But the truth is that it is also a future-based habit. Once the habit becomes addictive, the addict will seek to get his fix by any means necessary. A person will start out being a casual drug user. Eventually, he becomes so fixed on the drug that he will bankrupt himself to satisfy his addiction. The consequences of these actions will definitely affect his future and possibly those around him.

How many times have we seen successful people become homeless because of drug use? Drug use definitely becomes future based eventually. While we are in the mode of developing habits, we must look at where the habits are taking us. We will get more into this later on in the book when we deal with goal setting. What we need to do now is add more future-based habits to our daily lives.

Key points to remember when developing success habits:

- It all starts with a decision.

- Find the problem habits and fix them. You may need to work on one habit at a time based on your strength.

- Keep your eye on the prize. See yourself where you want to be and put knowledge and action into it.

- Remain consistent. You may want to make yourself accountable to someone. This will help, especially when the pain of change kicks in. You will need someone in your corner encouraging you.

- Repetition builds muscle. The more you do something, the better you become at it.

- Take baby steps out of your comfort zone, since stress and anxiety will kick in as you become uncomfortable. Giant steps will frustrate you and will zap you right back into the easy chair of your comfort zone. You really don't want this to happen because it would defeat the whole purpose. Taking baby steps will take you step by step towards excellence. Remember Aristotle's words of wisdom, "... excellence then, is not an act, but a habit'.

Also be sure to reward yourself with each successful habit that you develop. Never take your progress lightly. You've worked hard and you deserve a reward. Rewarding yourself will encourage you to move on to a higher level. Remember, the goal is excellence. Excellence is infinite. There is no end. You can always go higher.

CHAPTER 4

DO YOU NEED AN ATTITUDE ADJUSTMENT?

"Life is 10% what happens to me and 90% how I respond"
- Chuck Swindol

For most of us, our attitude depends on our current situation. If things are going great, we have a great attitude. If things are not looking so good, we have a not-so-good attitude. Unfortunately, the power of a good attitude is very underestimated. While it is human nature to act the way we feel, attitude is a difference maker. How we react to people and situations in life will determine how and where we end up. While action also plays a major role, having a positive attitude is very important to achieve any type of success. Let me break it down in story form.

Jack and Jim both worked for the local newspaper. They started at the company around the same time, department, and at the same level. To everyone, Jack seems to be a very lucky guy, always smiling and always with a joke or a word of encouragement for everyone.

On the surface, he seemed to be a problem-free guy without a care in the world. No matter what took place, or what seemed to go wrong in the department, Jack always had a solution or something encouraging to offer. Jim, on the other hand, constantly complained about everything that was going wrong. He would read the newspaper every morning and come to work complaining about what the government needed to do to fix everything that was going wrong, or he would make negative comments about everything going wrong with the country or even the company that he worked for. He complained about his salary, and he complained about not getting to work enough overtime so that he could make some extra money.

At one point, the company granted the department six months of overtime to complete an urgent time-sensitive project. Jim was instantly happy for the opportunity to make some extra money. Two weeks into the project he complained about being too tired because he had to work overtime all of the time, the same overtime that he constantly complained about not having. On the other hand, Jack made the best of the situation. In his mind, he welcomed the opportunity to not only make extra money, but he also saw it as a chance for him to learn more about the company and gain more experience. He instantly dismissed any form of tiredness or discomfort from his mind and focused on the benefits of being asked to work on such an important project.

Jack did his best to motivate Jim and explain to him that it was a learning experience and that the knowledge could take him to another level in the company. He explained to Jim that the six months would be over before he knew it and the extra money and learning opportunity, which were the benefits, would be worth the hard work. After a few weeks on the project, Jim gave into his negative thoughts and decided that he could no longer stress himself so he quit the project. Jack saw the project to completion, and even though he had twice as much work because he had to pick up Jim's slack, he was extremely grateful for the experience.

At the end of the project, Jack was awarded a certificate of participation by the corporate managers. A few months after that, his job performance was appraised and he was given a promotion to manage his department, not only because he completed the project single handedly, but because of his positive attitude. Unknowingly to Jack, his superiors had been observing his attitude for years and realized that not only was he extremely productive and a team player, he was also a problem solver. These personality traits made him a great asset to the company, and a winning candidate for promotion. Because Jim was the total opposite, he was left on the sidelines.

While most people will probably think that Jack was just in the right place at the right time or just lucky, the fact of the matter is that Jack's attitude got him promoted. Attitude is simply our way of reacting to life and its varying situations.

Develop the habit of a good attitude

Unfortunately, we have been programmed to believe that we must be happy when things are good and be down when things are down. The truth is that this practice was learned. It became a habit. As mentioned in the previous chapter, habits very often become involuntary and unconscious actions. We practice them so often that we perform the action without even being aware. We even fool ourselves into believing that this is just how situations are to be handled. Here's the thing: situations are handled the way we choose to handle them. We cannot control everything that happens to us in life. What we have complete control over is how we handle what happens to us. In order to have a winning attitude, we must deliberately develop the habit of a winning attitude.

While doing the research to write this book, I studied lots of successful motivational speakers like Steve Harvey and Les Brown. While they all had different ways of becoming successful, I observed that they all had winning attitudes. Many of the motivational speakers that I studied had the odds stacked against them. Many were written off as failures, and several came from poor and broken homes. The one thing that was consistent was their attitude toward their situation.

When reading their stories, I observed that most of them rose from the ashes; they got beat down time and time again by society and even their peers and family members, who tried desperately to keep them down inside the box from which they were trying to emerge. What I saw when I read their stories was their tenacity, their strong will, and their winning attitudes that were developed deliberately despite the odds. What do you see when you are encountered with a problem? Do you see it as a situation or do you see an opportunity? How you handle a challenge will determine your outcome.

A winning attitude can be practiced before an issue arises. Try to practice it daily. Develop the habit of smiling regularly even if there is nothing to smile about. Keep in mind that there are more things going right than wrong. Think of all of the good things that are happening. For example, if you have to clean your dishes, instead of griping about it, be thankful that you had food to eat off of those same dishes. Take it a step further and be thankful that you have dishes. Instead of griping about the house that you have to clean, be thankful that you have a house. Get into the habit of always seeing the good things in life. When you develop a good attitude toward the minor things, you are better able to handle the bigger challenges with a good attitude.

Don't waste valuable time having a bad attitude

Having a bad attitude about anything is a total waste of time and energy. Issues that are out of our control will always arise, and a bad attitude is rarely able to fix them. Being angry does not allow us to think rationally; therefore, a solution to the issue cannot be found. While it is human nature to become upset or disappointed when things don't go according to plan, the sooner we can get over our initial negative emotion and switch to a positive attitude, the sooner we can address the issue and seek a solution. Even if a solution is not found immediately, having a positive attitude makes the challenge easier to handle. Remaining positive enables us to get a broader perspective of the situation and seek better solutions.

A positive attitude is good for your health

Having a bad attitude for any reason causes stress. Stress affects not only the mind, but also the body. Temporary stress causes the body to get into fight or flight mode. When we practice and develop the habit of a negative attitude, we constantly put stress on the body. While this may not affect us initially, the repetition of it causes wear and tear on the body. High blood pressure and heart disease can be brought on by constant anger, fear, and depression. If you already suffer from these diseases, a constant bad attitude can compound these already dangerous health issues. Research has shown that when we practice handling situations in a positive manner and generally keep our environment positive, our well-being improves.

Believe it or not, negativity is contagious. Fortunately, so is positivity. Being in constant contact with positive people helps to keep our attitude that way. If we constantly associate with complainers, we will become contaminated by their attitudes and become complainers ourselves. A bad attitude helps NO ONE. Your attitude has the power to make or break you. YOU in turn have the power to determine if your attitude will make or break you. Whatever happens in your life, make the decision to weather it with a good attitude.

CHAPTER 5

TIME: HOW ARE YOU SPENDING IT?

"The bad news is time flies. The good news is you're the pilot"
- Michael Altshuler

As a stay-at-home mom, I also fell into the trap of being too busy. At the end of the day I was tired and frustrated with not much progress to show for it. I had recently resigned from my job to take care of my family and assist my husband with running a few of our home-based businesses. At this point, I had this grand idea that I was going to get more done because I did not have an eight hour job to take up my time. Boy, was I wrong about that one!

I quickly realized that without a game plan, working from home was no picnic. Over the years, I became more and more frustrated, since I just could not seem to balance my family life and business life. Each day was just one big unfinished mess, as one task seemed to run into the other or one task would overtake another. In my mind, there were always unfinished tasks, and new tasks popped up daily. Eventually, I got desperate and decided to seek some help. Unfortunately, what I learned is not taught in most schools, if any at all. The concept of time management is so unbelievably easy once it's put into practice and becomes a habit. There's that H word again. I must reiterate: Success is a habit that must be mastered through repetition. It is the simple things we do daily that will determine the direction we will go in life. When it comes to managing time, here are a few things that I learned and put into practice:

Everyone has the same 24 hours in a day

From the successful entrepreneur to the loafer, everyone is given the same amount of time on a daily basis. If you spend eight hours sleeping, eight hours on the job, and eight hours hanging out with the guys or girls, you have utilized your 24 hours by having an average day. If you spend eight hours sleeping, eight hours on the job, four hours relaxing or unwinding, and four hours socializing with successful and positive people, learning a trade or studying from a positive mental attitude book, you would have utilized your 24 hours investing in yourself and your future. Be very careful how and where you spend your time. It's not how much time you have, it's what you do with it that counts.

The biggest mistake that is made where time is concerned is believing that it will always be there or that it moves very slowly. Time is very subtle. Lots of it can slip away unnoticed. Because life can be the same day by day, the monotony of it can deceive the masses into believing that time is always on our side and that there is no need to rush when making plans for the future. When constructing a game plan, it is very critical to keep in mind that days turn into months and months turn into years at an alarming rate. It's very easy to fall into the trap of relaxing and thinking that there is enough time to put game plans in place. The phrase 'time flies when you're having fun' is right on target. The time to get busy is NOW. Remember, procrastination is a killer.

Time is money

The trick is to make every second count. When learning to budget our income, we were taught to give every dollar a name. We were told to take one month and track every dollar. Everything we spent had to be recorded. At the end of that month, we had to study the record to see where our money was going every month. By paying careful attention, we realized that money was being spent unnecessarily in certain areas.

For example, we were paying monthly gym fees and not being consistent with attending the gym. By making a record of our spending, we were able to see where our budget was leaking money and stop the leaks.

It's the same thing with time management. I had to make a record of the things that I did on a daily basis to figure out where my time was going. So I need you to try this. Every day for one week, record what you do on an hourly basis, from the time you get out of bed, to the time that you go to bed. It may be a bit of a task but bear with me. It will be worth it. There are times that you may even forget to log a few entries, but try as much as possible to keep up with it for 1 week. This log must be made during your normal days and not when you are doing something out of the ordinary like taking vacation or going on business leave.

If you are a student, then you must do this while you are at school and not when you are on vacation leave. After your log is made, study it carefully and see exactly where your time is going. Maybe you spend an hour every day on social media. Maybe you spend two hours every day on the phone discussing people and their lives. If you are honest with yourself, you will see where you need to cut out the extra non-productive time and apply it somewhere productive.

Time is like money. It is spent daily. Just like we can decide what we spend our money on, we can decide what we spend our time on. If you spend one hour cleaning the kitchen, at the end of that one hour, you would have bought yourself a clean kitchen. Just as time can be used to purchase tangible things like a clean kitchen, it can also be used to purchase non-tangible things. If you spend half of your day playing a video game that enacts violence, twelve hours later, you would have purchased a somewhat violent mind. If most of your time is spent perfecting or mastering this, in the long run, more violence would be purchased and deposited in your mind.

What if you decide to spend most of your free time reading books and watching videos about successful habits like proper time management and a positive attitude? You would be purchasing winning information that will be deposited in your mind. Once this deposit is made into your mind bank, winning actions will then follow. Activities that time is spent on daily will determine what purchases we end up with in the future. Be careful what you buy with your time. Unlike money, once time is spent, there is no refund.

The difference between being productive and being busy

Don't confuse the two. If you are constantly bombarded with tasks that seem to be never-ending, and at the end of the day you have completed basically nothing, you are too busy.

Being busy and accomplishing nothing only leads to frustration and, eventually, a bad attitude. You may accomplish a few things when you're busy, but the question to ask yourself is 'Was I productive?' In order to become productive, you need to have an idea of everything that needs to get done and then prioritize your tasks.

Learn to prioritize with a TO DO list

In his book *"4 Secrets So You Can Win Everyday"*, Vicente Cotto explains the importance of mastering the success habit of using a TO DO list on purpose every day. Your list should be made at a time when you are able to think clearly. For some people, this is at bedtime; for others, it is first thing in the morning. Here is what he recommends:

- Make a list of everything that needs to be done. Make the list on paper, and not in your head. Write it down. This is called your 'brain dump' list.

- From this list, your TO DO list will be made. Select from your 'dump' list the 4 - 7 most important tasks that MUST get done today. These tasks must be high on the 'critical' scale.

- Stick to 4 - 7 tasks so that you do not feel overwhelmed when you look at your list.

- Of those 4 to 7 tasks, at least 1 - 2 of them should be tasks that will take you closer to your future goals.

The act of adding 1 or 2 future-based tasks to your list is exceptionally genius, as it takes you 1 or 2 steps closer to your future success. Taking 2 steps daily toward that success will get you 60 steps closer in one month. Too often, we tend to think that future success starts in the future. It starts NOW. Future success is in your daily habits.

As you go through your day and complete the tasks on your TO DO list, be sure to check them off. This will give you a sense of accomplishment. At the end of the day, you will see what you spent your time doing instead of wondering where the day went. If you are able to complete everything on your TO DO list with time to spare, you can allow yourself to go back to your dump list and select one or two more tasks. This, of course, is optional, but I would strongly suggest that you call it a day and take the free time that you have now accomplished to do something fun. It is extremely important that you reward yourself for your accomplishment. This allows you to balance your life with work time and play time.

Working with a TO DO list will take some time to master. You may fall back into your old habit a few times before mastering the new habit, but the trick is to make the decision daily to practice it ON PURPOSE. This successful habit is well worth the effort as it eases the frustration of trying to conquer the world of tasks daily, and it allows you to be productive and not busy. After practicing and developing this habit myself, I am totally convinced that it is absolutely unnecessary for any free human being to be inundated with tasks unless they choose to be.

Learn to share (the work-load)

Learn to delegate. There is no law that states that in order for someone to become successful, they must shoulder all of the workload. Bill Gates does not run Microsoft all by himself. Neither does Richard Branson fly solo at Virgin Atlantic. In fact, these men probably are hardly seen at the office. These successful men know that the thing to do is to work smart and not work hard. They build an efficient team around themselves, and all of the work gets shared with the team. Each team member has a specific task.

If you find yourself overwhelmed with work, delegate certain tasks to others. You may find someone who has a talent for a particular task that you loathe. Just simply shift that task to that 'expert'. This will free you up to do other things more efficiently. When you juggle too many things, you tend to do things less than perfectly and end up frustrated.

Once you have delegated the work and things are running smoothly, allow things to run smoothly. Too often, I have seen people try to micro-manage others when things are going well. It makes absolutely no sense to ask for help steering the ship and still steer the ship from a distance. Sharing the workload should enable you to get more done in less time with better quality results.

Proper time management is not rocket-science or brain surgery. All it takes is a little practice to develop the habit. Once the habit is mastered, it's smooth sailing.

Managing time is critical. As I mentioned earlier, time once spent has no refund. Time is infinite. It never ends, but unfortunately, we do. Do everything that needs to be done while you're living. Time is precious. Don't waste a second of it.

CHAPTER 6

READY, SET GOALS!

"Goals are dreams with deadlines" - Diana Scharf Hunt

So what is your game plan? Have you identified what it is that you want in life? Have you decided how you are going to go about getting it? Achieving your dreams or game plan requires goal setting.

A goal is simply a plan of action to get a task done to achieve success. If you want to lose weight but put no plan of action in place to follow, you will not lose a single pound. Almost nothing moves forward without a plan. Your life will not automatically fall into place without goals. If you want to get out of debt but change absolutely nothing about your spending habits, you will remain in debt. This seems like simple common sense, but the amazing thing is that most people seriously believe that life will get better later on without making a move to make it better. The harsh reality is that if you do nothing to make things better, that's exactly what you will get—NOTHING!

For some reason, we look at people who have achieved success and think that they got there automatically. Trust me, they did not. They set goals and put plans in place. Time and time again we hear of people climbing Mount Everest. One thing that we must realize is that they did not just automatically appear or land on the summit. They had to put plans in place and work hard to get there. Like time management, goal setting is not rocket science or brain surgery; all it takes is some planning and discipline.

Decide what you what to accomplish

This is just the beginning. It may take some thought and sometime but close your eyes and visualize where you want to be five years from now. In your mind it may seem like a stretch or a huge step to get from where you are now to where you'd like to be five years later, but do not allow this to deter you. We were not created to dream big for nothing. When we were children, nothing stopped us from being the best and biggest success in our minds 'when we grow up'. Whatever it is that you want in life, get a success journal and write it down. Yes! Write it down. If it's the dream house that you want, put a picture of it on your mirror, or someplace that you can see every day. This is where success starts: in your mind. Next, determine that you are getting this done, whatever it is.

Break it down

In order to make a huge goal seem attainable, it must be broken down into smaller goals. A long-term goal must be broken down into short-term goals. If you have a five-year goal, break it down (on paper) into five one-year goals. Then break each one-year goal into smaller goals like monthly goals. Take it one step at a time. A house is not built in one day. Construction may take a few months depending on the size. First the foundation is built, then the walls, then the roof. It's the same thing with your goals. Write down every step on paper. This is your life plan, so take it seriously.

Make each short-term goal realistic. If you know that you cannot put in 12 hours per day to work on your goal, do not write it down. You may be able to accomplish that for the first few days, but, eventually, you will burn yourself out and quite possibly abandon your goals. It is far better to realistically put in one hour every day and achieve some progress than to force yourself to do far more than you can and then jump ship before you're halfway through your journey. Like your 'to do' list, be sure to check off every baby step that you have completed. Every baby step takes you closer to accomplishing your long-term goal. Remember to reward yourself for every bite-sized goal that you have completed. DO NOT give up. Keep taking the baby steps. It will be worth it.

Make yourself accountable to someone who will encourage you every step of the way. It's really important to have someone in your corner when the 'growing pains' of stretching your comfort zone start to kick in and you're tempted to give up.

Detour?!

There are times in life when things do not go according to our perfectly laid plans. Let's face it—life happens. When we are going along the road to success, there are times when we encounter a roadblock. We may have a setback because of illness. Whatever happens, we need to be resilient. Things may slow us down a little, but we must NEVER allow these unforeseen life events to stop us from accomplishing our dreams. Every single successful person has encountered setbacks in some form or other. The one thing that all of these people have in common is that they did not quit. I am quite sure that the thought crossed their mind, but they did not give in to it. Setbacks and challenges are simply a part of success. They are a part of your growing process. Learn to master the art of handling them. Here are some tips on how to bounce back when you encounter challenges:

See it as a challenge and learn from it

Refuse to believe that this happened to destroy you. Every experience in life should teach us something. Refuse to dwell in self-pity. Self-pity is a crippling stagnant action. Get over it FAST! Instead of asking why this happened to you, ask yourself what you can learn from it. Once you get over this setback and learn from it, you will become stronger. You will be prepared for whatever comes next.

DO NOT play the blame game

While it may suit you to point fingers and lay blame on someone, refuse to waste time with that. It may very well be someone's fault, possibly even yours, but at this point, the damage is already done. Unless the damage can be undone, or the spilled milk miraculously becomes un-spilled, it's time to move forward. Precious time has already been lost; don't waste another precious second or valuable energy holding up progress. Refuse to become preoccupied with setbacks. Refuse to become the victim.

Get creative

It's very important to note that an obstacle in the road is not the end. If the obstacle is too big to be moved or maneuvered, take a detour. It may take longer to get to the destination, but the key is to not put the success vehicle permanently in park or make a U-turn and head for home. There may be many other roads that lead to your goal. You may need to get creative and take the longer, more scenic route. The detour could even possibly be a shortcut in disguise. The road to success is not a straight road. It has twists and turns, steep inclines and dips. It has roadblocks and, yes, detours. DO NOT ever abandon your dreams or your goals because things don't go the way you expect them to. Just as there will be setbacks and detours, things will also happen in your favor.

Your goals are the bite-sized pieces that you take to consume the entire elephant that is your dream. If you look at the entire elephant, you will think it impossible to consume the entire thing. Breaking it down into pieces will make it attainable.

Keep moving

At the end of it all, after all of your bite-sized goals have been accomplished and you step back and take a look at the masterpiece of your long-term goal that you have finally accomplished, please be sure to congratulate yourself on a job well done. Just as you rewarded yourself every time you completed a short-term goal, you MUST reward yourself big-time for this one. Take the time to appreciate and bask in the glory of your accomplishment.

Your hard work and determination has finally paid off. At this point, you should now be able to convince yourself that you can move mountains. However, as much as you have finally accomplished your dreams, do not allow your dreams to end there. You are just beginning. Continue to dream big. Never allow yourself to think that you have 'arrived'. If you do, you will be once again limiting yourself and your potential by allowing this new level to become a comfort zone. Like the sky, success has no limits, so once again, step out of your bigger box and conquer new territory.

Just like you put a plan of action or game plan in place to get to your new level of success, you can now put a plan of action together to get even further. On your new level, you are now able to meet new people from whom you can learn. Always use every opportunity to learn from those around you. Never assume or believe that you know it all. Learning is infinite. It never ends.

DONNETTE'S STORY

At age 23, Donnette made the big decision to migrate from her native St. Vincent to the island of Antigua. Jobs were scarce at the time, so the decision to leave in search of a better life would appear to be a no-brainer. However, her situation was not as 'cut and dry'. She was not only the single parent of a 3-year-old daughter, but she was also expecting her second child. Where most people would accept their current situation and hope for the best, she left her daughter in her sister's care and set off in search of a better life with a plan to send for her daughter when she got settled. Upon her arrival in Antigua, she was able to find temporary work, but because she had not completed her high school education, the jobs were menial. In Donnette's mind, her situation was only temporary and no job was too small or degrading. Her motto was 'it's not where you are, it's where you're going'.

It was shortly after the birth of her second child that she was offered a job at a school as the maid. While working there, she used the opportunity to teach herself basic computer skills with the help of her employer. Every spare moment that she had was used reading books from the school's library. Very soon, she was able to comprehend the school's curriculum and learning program. Within a year, she learned the program so well that she was asked to teach it to the new teachers that came on staff.

Donnette also took classes to complete her high school education. Three years later, she was offered a teaching position at the school for the first- and second-year nursery students. While teaching, she realized that if she was going to teach others, she herself needed to continue her education because, as she said, 'you cannot teach what you do not know'. Throughout her years of teaching at this school, she continued to take extra classes, and it was not long before she achieved her degree in Early Childhood Education.

After earning her degree, she realized her true passion was teaching and continued to upgrade herself by enrolling in evening classes at a local church-based school, which was not too far away from where she taught. Unknown to her, the officials at that school were closely monitoring her progress and were quite impressed with her. One day, she received a call from the principal there. He explained that they had been perusing her files and were quite impressed with her hard work, dedication, and passion for teaching. They then offered her the position of vice principal at their school. Although she felt an obligation to her current employers at the time, with their blessings and well wishes, she made the decision to move forward. While fulfilling her new role at her new job, she realized that her knowledge in education was not enough, as her role in that administrative field entailed a bit of business knowledge in terms of running a school, so she enrolled in business administration classes. A few years later, she earned her degree in business and education.

Donnette is now putting steps in place to continue her education and upgrade herself on a yearly basis. Although she faces challenges like everyone else, she refuses to accept obstacles as defeat or make excuses. She believes that in order to be successful, you must have a plan in place and stick to it. Looking back on where she has come from and what she has accomplished, she uses her story to motivate and encourage others, including her children.

She is now married with four children who have learned from this tremendously determined woman, and who, like their mother, believe in setting goals and eliminating all excuses.

CHAPTER 7

WINDING DOWN

"The time for action is now. It's never too late to do something" - Antoine de Saint-Exupery

Unfortunately, most of us believe the lie we tell ourselves that it's too late to make a move to progress in life. We convince ourselves that we're too old, we've missed our opportunities, or the time for greatness has passed, and on and on we go with the excuses. NEWSFLASH!! Success does not only apply to the young, and to this day, dreams have no expiration dates. Success is for everyone. Every piece of advice that I have shared with you in this book applies to both young and old. Not everyone peaks in their twenties or thirties. There are lots of us who 'got it' a long time after most people did.

The smart thing to do is to stop wasting precious time on regrets and use the time that we now have to progress. Instead of seeing the glass half empty at this stage and lamenting over the youth that we no longer have on our side, let's see the glass half full and focus on what we have left and what we have achieved over the years that we can now put to good use.

Late achievers have quite a few things going in their favor. One of the things that they have on their side is experience. They have lived longer and therefore experienced more of life, from different personalities to different life challenges. With experience comes wisdom. They are better at troubleshooting because of experiences that they have learned from over the years. Once a late achiever 'gets it', they are eager to start the ball rolling as they realize that too many unproductive years have passed. This is a real asset as it motivates them to keep the ball rolling and stay focused. Also, at this stage, they are well past the 'partying' phase and are less distracted by social activities that may take away from their productivity.

They are less tolerant of petty and time-wasting issues that may tend to distract the younger person. If you are a late achiever, these are some of the many benefits that you have to make a start. Concentrate on these assets and the many others that you have and use them as your ladder to success.

Use your tools

We were all born with different gifts, talents, and desires. The different gifts that we have all contribute to making the world go around. We can't all be doctors, and we can't all be rocket scientists. Each of us has just the right talents and gifts that we need to get us to where we need to go. Of course, we can learn from each other and develop new talents, but the key thing to know is that no one is useless unless he or she chooses to be.

Another thing to be careful of is comparing ourselves to others. While we strive for excellence, we sometimes tend to use others as a measuring stick. This can be beneficial if we see others as positive role models who we choose to emulate. However, if we are going to belittle ourselves because we do not measure up to our mentors, this may not be a good habit to develop.

It is important to be in a constant state of growth and learning, but at the same time, we need to keep in mind that we are all different, we all grow at different rates, and our skills and gifts are not always the same. If your mentor is way ahead of you in terms of where you want to be in life, bear in mind that they may have been practicing success habits way before you began, and their experience is the reason you may have sought them out in the first place.

You go where you are focused and whatever you are focused on grows

Critical to success is how focused we are on our goals and dreams. Once the goal is set, it becomes vitally important to your dream that your focus remains on the goal. It's very easy to become distracted by life's ups and downs. Let's face it. Things were taking place before we put our game plan together, and things will continue to take place as we execute our plans. Life will happen, the earth will continue to rotate on its axis, the children will continue to grow, the sun will rise and set, and on and on life will go. It's really amazing the excuses we come up with to ditch our game plan or to put our goals on hold because the same things that were happening before we decided to take our future seriously are still happening.

I am simply saying that we should never have the misconception that because we have taken a step in the right direction, all of life would miraculously be perfect. We should be aware that there may be setbacks, but we should also make up our minds to remain focused on where we are headed. The car may break down, someone may become ill, and there may be job losses, but we should always keep our eyes on where we are headed. There may be times when our game plan may need to be altered or postponed for a short while, but, whatever you do, NEVER EVER quit the plan. If you quit, then you lose. One thing that is sure to haunt you is a game plan that has never been completed. It haunts the victim for life. It is far better to complete it and fail than to start it and never complete it.

Failures that occur after completion should never be considered failures; they are valuable experiences from which you learn and grow. Be sure to expect the bumps in the road and the twists and turns. It's just the way of life.

Eliminate distractions

Distractions can and will come in many forms. Temporary distractions happen daily and almost every second on the second. Text messages, email notifications, telephone calls ... the list goes on and on. If you are a person who can multitask and work through these constant distractions, kudos to you.

For the rest of us, we may need to put some measures in place to avoid being distracted. It helps tremendously to put your phone on silent or turn off your notifications while you complete a task or goal. Setting up a daily schedule is another vital habit to develop. For example, checking and responding to emails can be done at a particular time in the day and returning calls that were missed because the phone was on silent while a task was being completed can also be scheduled.

You can also get creative with your schedule and set it to suit your tasks. For example, if you have a weakness for social media, after you have completed your first few goals for the day, you can now reward yourself by allowing yourself an extra 10 minutes or so to check your newsfeed. Social media can be very entertaining and addictive, but be sure to limit the amount of time you spend on it as it can become a huge distraction. I have experienced first-hand how minutes can turn to hours, and before you know it, practically the whole day is spent on this present-based activity, and not one minute is spent on a future-based activity.

Whatever your distractions are, find ways to eliminate them. If you cannot fully eliminate them, then create a habit of bringing them under your control. If you do not, then they will control you and your future. When preparing your 'TO DO' list, always think of the distractions that will most likely appear to halt your progress. Once you can identify the distraction or obstacle, put a plan in place to overcome or eliminate it. Always be prepared with a plan of action to counteract every distraction. Some of them we see coming before they appear, so prepare for those with a plan to shoot them down. You know your weaknesses. Prepare for them.

Permanent distractions can be your peers. Be very careful of your associations while activating your game plan. If the people you associate with are not on board with your plan, it may be a wise idea to put them aside and associate with those who are on board. Unfortunately, the reality is that most people who are on the same level as you and have no plan to elevate themselves are never in favour of you elevating yourself.

As I mentioned earlier in this book, they may even sound like they mean well, and they probably do when they try to dissuade you from stepping out of your comfort zone. These distractions will be very difficult to eliminate, since they are most likely loved ones. I am in no way telling you to ostracize yourself from these people. But you will definitely need to spend less time associating with them and more time focusing on your goals. To prove the naysayers wrong, you must succeed.

No inspiration? No problem

It's not every day that you are going to feel like 'doing' success. In fact, most days you probably may not feel like it. If everybody felt like being successful, we all would be. If you ask the greatest achievers if they were in the mood every day, they would tell you the same thing. Most times they just did not feel like practicing the habits that made them successful. They felt the urge to quit when things got tough. But they persevered. I can honestly tell you that while writing this book, there were days that I did not feel like writing it. I had no inspiration. But guess what? All it took was for me to sit at the desk anyway and start writing.

Little by little, the feeling came, and before I knew it, I had a chapter or two completed. What I learned from this experience was that inspiration will catch up once you start the work. Never allow yourself to become stagnant because you did not 'feel like' doing something. Develop the habit of doing it anyway. Progress can never be made if you do nothing.

Knowing is ONLY half the battle won

Knowledge is power. But it's only brain power. If you never put what you learn or know into action, you are just as powerful as if you knew nothing. The key to success is not only knowledge; it's knowledge AND action. A gym membership is no good unless it is used. A doctor can have a degree in neurology, but if he does not practice in that field, whether teaching or otherwise, that degree is useless. If after reading this book you do not apply the information that I shared, then all you have gained is just information. Doing a little each day is better than doing nothing at all. Being consistent will eventually pay off in the long run.

Here is another thing that I learned: The simple things that are done daily will have an effect, no matter what they are. If all you eat daily is junk, you will not see the results immediately. After a few months or years, however, your health will definitely reflect your poor choices. Similarly, if your quest is to lose a few pounds and you eat healthy meals and exercise daily, you will not see changes immediately, but after a few months, you will certainly see the results. Every action has a result.

Consistent small actions have small results daily, but each small result will add up to a big result, whether good or bad. With success, if one success action yielded immediate success, everyone would have no problem doing what it takes.

That is the problem with our 'microwave society'. We need to see quick results. If we don't, then we decide that 'it's not working'. Let's use the analogy of a smoker. Everyone knows that cigarettes can cause lung and other cancers. Even the smokers know that. So, if they know that, why do they continue to smoke? Simple. Because they know that it will not kill them instantly. If it did, then no one without a death wish would ever smoke.

Similarly, if eating a greasy burger and fries would cause one to have an instant heart attack, or instantly become morbidly obese, no one would touch the stuff. It takes probably years of these actions for these consequences to catch up. Okay, so one cigarette won't kill you and one burger won't morph you into a 300-pound person. It takes months and years to get that result. It's the same thing with success. Months and years of consistent action will bring your goals to completion.

This is why it is so critical to stay the course and remain true to your success habits. This particular habit is the most important one to develop. Human beings do not grow to the size of an adult in one day. Day by day, a baby grows, and the results are seldom seen on a day-to-day basis, since the changes are very subtle. Consistent daily action is the key habit for any success. Mastering this success habit is worth more than its weight in gold.

Avoid living in the Museum of You

As mentioned earlier in this book, once your goal is accomplished, be sure to reward yourself. However, never allow yourself to get too comfortable with your accomplishments. Always see yourself moving forward. Too often, many people get comfortable with whatever progress they have made and stay there. Don't fall into the trap of getting there and staying there and for decades on end talking constantly about your great accomplishments that took place eons ago.

Absolutely nothing is wrong with that if you wish to remain at the same spot for the remainder of your natural life. Then, by all means, your decision should be respected. However, if you wish to continue to achieve, the universe is the limit. Earvin 'Magic' Johnson, who played point guard for the LA Lakers, is a great example of someone who refuses to live in a museum. He won championship after championship during his basketball career. But after retiring from the NBA, he kept progressing. He has since become an entrepreneur, motivational speaker, and broadcaster, among many other things.

In 2009, Ebony Magazine named him one of America's most influential black businessmen. He also owns numerous businesses, and the list of his accomplishments goes on and on. Based on his trends, it seems to me that we will be hearing about his constant successes for decades to come. There are many other greats like Mr. Johnson who are constantly on the move, attaining great things year after year. Try to be an upgrade of yourself every year if possible. Keep learning and keep growing.

Who's marking your test paper?

Everyone learns from everyone. Who are you learning from? Who is learning from you? Everyone should be accountable to someone. If we are going to be learning success habits, we should be learning them from successful people who are where we want to be in life. Once you have found that person or persons, they become your mentors. They are the ones who should be marking your test paper, checking your progress and guiding your steps. When choosing a mentor, I strongly recommend that the choice is made based on several things.

- Check the integrity of the individual. Unless you are choosing a path down a dark road, I recommend that you choose someone with morals and scruples, someone who not only talks the talk, but someone who also walks it.

- While you can have more than one mentor, the key person mentoring you should have a vast knowledge of the field that you wish to enter, or have the lifestyle that you wish to have. Also, different mentors can be extremely beneficial as everyone has different experiences and strengths in different areas that you can learn from. One may have profound business skills; another can have great motivational skills. Put yourself in a position to learn from everyone.

- Avoid mentors that are bossy, critical, and disrespectful. Your mentor should have your best interest at heart. While they may not agree with everything that you do or say, correction should never be cruel or disrespectful. Your mentor should be your mentor and not your dictator.

- Know exactly what you want in a mentor. If you are not too sure, you should be able to test a few to see how the relationship goes and determine if they are who you are looking for. Have conversations to ensure that you have found someone who is the right fit for you. Always be honest and upfront. Let the individual know what you are looking for.

As mentioned earlier, some mentors may not have all of the qualities that you seek, but if they have even a few, take the opportunity to learn from them. A mentor is someone you should learn from. Once you receive information from him or her, you should start applying the knowledge.

Do not expect your mentor to be constantly pushing you to do whatever he or she recommends. If you are not ready for action, then I suggest that you defer the process of mentorship until you are ready, as you do not want to waste your mentor's time and services. Some mentors will tell you that they do not work with any and everyone for this very reason.

Mentorship is a relationship that involves trust, and that trust should work in both directions. A mentor is also a teacher. Guess what? Everyone is a mentor. Everyone is teaching someone something. What are you teaching others? Your life is a lesson that others learn from. Are you using your life to teach others how to succeed or how to fail?

Ask yourself that question. If you don't like the answer, then do something to change it.

Leave a legacy

Everyone, when they depart this earth, leaves a legacy for the future generations. What legacy are you leaving? Once you have learned to improve yourself, you are now required to teach others. This is the only way that our society will make the change from negative to positive. The appeal that I make is loud and strong.

We live in a society where there are lots of confused and depressed people who don't know how to go up in life because of the negative role models that they had. Guess what? These people are now the role models for the present and future generations. I don't know about you, but for me, it's a scary situation. Instead of writing people off, we need to get our minds educated on the greatness within us and teach it not only to the younger generation but to everyone we know who needs it.

Positive role models are needed to educate the masses and to change the direction of many lives headed the wrong way. Success is only useful to a certain point. Without a successor, it will eventually die. Your success must make a difference not only in your life but also in the lives of others. Let's reach out to the masses. Let's launch *Operation Game Plan* and teach others to do the same.

CONCLUSION ● ● ● ● ● ● ● ● ● ● ● ● ● ● ● ● ●

"If you can't fly, then run, it you can't run, then walk, if you can't walk, then crawl, but whatever you do, you have to keep moving forward." - Martin Luther King Jr.

Knowledge is power, but it is only powerful once action is applied to it. Everyone has that greatness within. Reach deep into yourself and pull it out. No fear or excuses. It is my hope that this book will assist you on your path to your dreams and beyond.

Believe in you. You are more than worth it!

You have that gift to contribute that the world needs. Don't fall asleep on your dreams. They are worth too much. Make the decision to move forward and to keep moving forward.

Those who sleep, remain in their comfort zone.

WHILE YOU WERE SLEEPING • • • • • • • •

While you were sleeping, I was awake,

I had no real pain, but there was an ache,

That ache was frustration of life remaining the same,

Day in and day out, there was no claim to fame.

No plan for the future, no plan for success,

To put it quite bluntly, my life was a mess.

A mess by my standards was a great life for most,

I had a 'safe job', and a family to boast.

Mediocrity plays games on the minds that conform,

And follow the masses who think it's the norm,

To live by existing to pay bills and die,

Day in and day out, we all believed the lie.

It was then I decided, and this might sound strange,

That things needed to change by me making a change.

A change in my mindset, a change in my words,

A change in my vision, a change in my voice.

After years of conforming to the same average habits,

I made a decision and made off like a bandit.

With positive mentors and books that taught facts

Of the greatness within me I never could see.

After years of brainwashing and mental abuse,

From the hands of society that served negative news,

I made off like a bandit with positive food

That I chose to eat daily from positive feeds.

Negative role models, negative friends, negative habits and negative trends

Are all now replaced with success-minded brands.

My mind can see clearly where its vision was once banned.

While you were sleeping, the new branded me

Has made the decision to toil tirelessly

Using every positive thing I have learned,

I'll apply it to action so results I will earn.

As knowledge can only be useful, you see,

When backed up with action and hard work purposely.

So while you were sleeping, I've become a success,

A different person from the girl that was a mess,

My new goals are set and I now have a plan

To raise up a people, a successful clan.

I'll teach what I've learned, leave a legacy, now I can;

I'll teach you to launch your *Operation Game Plan*.

- Chrys-Ann Ambrose

Your current actions predict your future.
What does your future hold? You choose.

ABOUT THE AUTHOR

Chrys-Ann Ambrose lives on the Caribbean island of Antigua and is a stay-at-home mom whose passion is taking care of her husband, Colin, and her two daughters, Tiara and Jewel.

Apart from assisting her husband with running several home-based businesses, she enjoys writing and giving motivational talks to those who need it.

She admits that she was not always a positive person, but after years of reading positive mental attitude books and studying motivational videos, her mindset has changed dramatically, and with that, her life changed, too. Chrys-Ann has spent the last 5 years sharing positive information with many, and her goal is to launch her career as a professional motivational speaker.

Lookout for great things in the very near future from this author.

WE WANT TO HEAR FROM YOU!!!

If this book has made a difference in your life Chrys-Ann would be delighted to hear about it.

Leave a review on Amazon.com!

BOOK CHRYS-ANN TO SPEAK AT YOUR NEXT EVENT!

Send an email to: booking@publishyourgift.com

Learn more about Chrys-Ann at:

www.ChrysAnnAmbrose.com

FOLLOW CHRYS-ANN ON SOCIAL MEDIA

f Chrys-AnnAmbrose   ChrysAmbrose

"EMPOWERING YOU TO IMPACT GENERATIONS"

WWW.PUBLISHYOURGIFT.COM

CPSIA information can be obtained
at www.ICGtesting.com
Printed in the USA
LVOW04s0701030116
468871LV00001B/1/P